I0484845

Mount Forest Ontario in Colour Photos, Saving Our History One Photo at a Time

Photography
by Barbara Raué
2015

Series Name:
Cruising Ontario

Book 96: Mount Forest

Cover photo: Post Office

Series Name: Cruising Ontario
Saving Our History One Photo at a Time
in colour photos

Other Books by Barbara Raue

Coins of Gold

Arrows, Indians and Love

The Life and Times of Barbara
Volume 1: Inventions That Have Enhanced My Life
Volume 2: Entertainment That I Have Enjoyed
Volume 3: East Coast Trips
Volume 4: Olympics Have Always Intrigued Me
Volume 5: Wonders of the World
Volume 6: Caribbean Cruises We Have Enjoyed
Volume 7: Animals
Volume 8: Storms and Other Major Disasters in My Lifetime
Volume 9: Wars, Terrorist Attacks and Major Disasters

The Cromwell Family Book

Laura Secord Discovered

Visit Barbara's website to view all of her books
http://barbararaue.ca

Mount Forest

Mount Forest is located at the junction of Highways 6 and 89 on a height of land near the headwaters of the Saugeen River. In 1871, eighteen years after the town was surveyed, it had ten hotels, eight churches and eighteen stores; the first train came into Mount Forest later that year.

Prior to European settlement, present day Mount Forest was prime hunting ground for the Saugeen Ojibway peoples due to its location on the Saugeen River.

Originally known as Maitland Hills, its name was changed to Mount Forest in 1853. The name change came about because it was discovered that the village was actually on the Saugeen River system not on the Maitland River as had previously been supposed.

The village was surveyed into lots in 1853. By 1864, the population had grown to 1185 so that it qualified to be incorporated as a village. By 1879 it had become an incorporated town. The 1871 town directory stated that Mount Forest had ten hotels, eight churches and eighteen stores. Later that year the railway was completed and the first train entered Mount Forest pulled by a wood-burning engine.

A local newspaper, the *Mount Forest Confederate*, was first printed in 1867. For the first year, the newspaper was sent to village residents free of charge, but the second year it began charging 50 cents per year.

The first public school was built in 1856. The first high school was originally in the Old Drill Hall, but was an unsuitable location because it was beside the Market Square where livestock sales were held monthly. The new high school was built in 1878. A third high school was founded in 2004 with the combination of the Mount Forest District High school and the neighboring Town of Arthur.

Dr. A.R. Perry purchased the home of Alex Martin on the corner of Dublin and Princess Streets and established Strathcona Hospital, a 10-bed private hospital. In 1923, a group of citizens headed by G.L. Allen, changed Strathcona Hospital into a public hospital. Wentworth Marshall, a pharmacist, generously bought the hospital from Perry. Marshall's mother, Louise, was the supervisor at the hospital until she became ill with cancer. It was closed in 1921, but a year later reopened under a new name: Mount Forest General Hospital. In 1928, the deed of the hospital was turned over to the town and the name was changed yet again to Louise Marshall Hospital in honour of Marshall's mother.

Mount Forest was amalgamated into the new township of Wellington North on January 1, 1999.

Gobles

Gobles is located on concession 1 of Blenheim Township about two miles west of Princeton. In 1855 Gobles Corners was named after the late William L. Goble, son of Rev. Jacob Goble, who came to Canada from New York State in 1811 and settled on Concession 1 of Blenheim Township about 1816. Jacob Goble was elected first Deacon of the Blenheim Free Communion Church (Baptist) in 1822. He kept the office in his general store on the west side of the Blenheim Township three quarter town line near the G.W.R. tracks at Gobles. He held the position until December 19, 1873 when he resigned.

When the railway was built the station bore the name "Gobles". A post office was established at Gobles on July 1, 1855, with William L. Goble as postmaster with a mail route begun between Gobles Corners and Princeton. Alex Milmine made one trip per week for two months between July and September 1855. This route was continued by W. L. Goble until September 30, 1858. Two trips per week were made by horse or vehicle. Between September 30, 1858 and September 30, 1863, the pay was $50.00 per year for two trips per week. William L. Goble also had the contract for mail conveying from Gobles Corners post office to the railway station. Twelve trips per week were made for two months in 1859 and 1860 and again in September 1863 in connection with the travelling post office.

For nine months commencing October 1, 1863, Jasper G. Goble carried mail on foot six times per week from the Gobles Corners post office to the railway station for which he received $37.00. He continued this for four years until 1867. Jasper G. Goble was the son of William L. Goble. He became postmaster on April 1, 1874 and resigned on August 15, 1896. The population in 1875 was 50. The name of the post office was changed to Gobles on November 1, 1895.

All of the postmasters kept the post office in the same general store started by W. L. Goble. The last postmaster at Gobles was B. J. Force, farmer, thresher, storekeeper, from April 23, 1912 to May 1, 1940, when the office was closed. Gobles then became part of the rural mail delivery on R.R. No. 1 Princeton.

Table of Contents

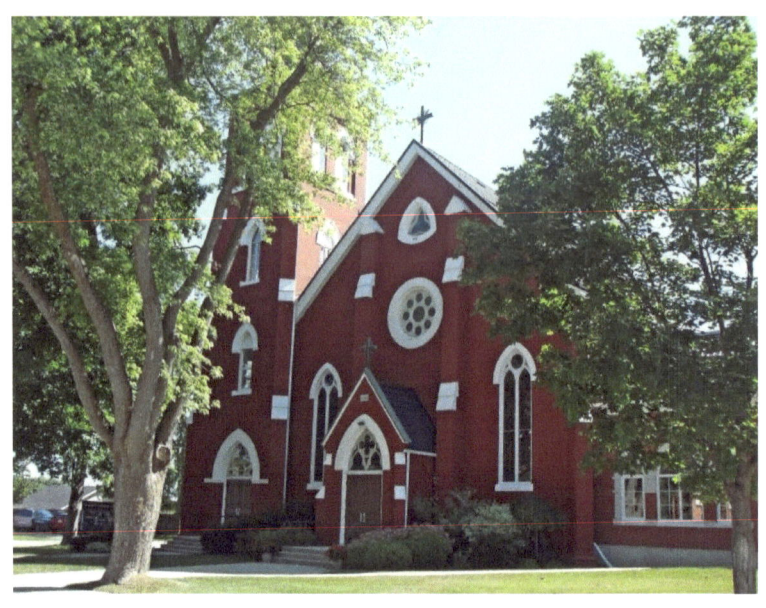

230 Queen Street East - St. Mary's Catholic Church
established 1863 – buttresses, lancet windows, dichromatic

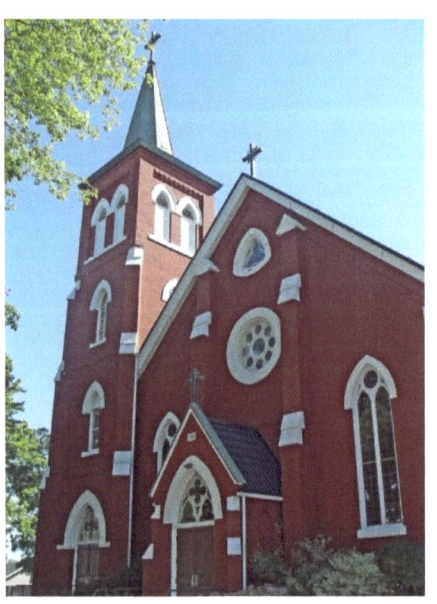

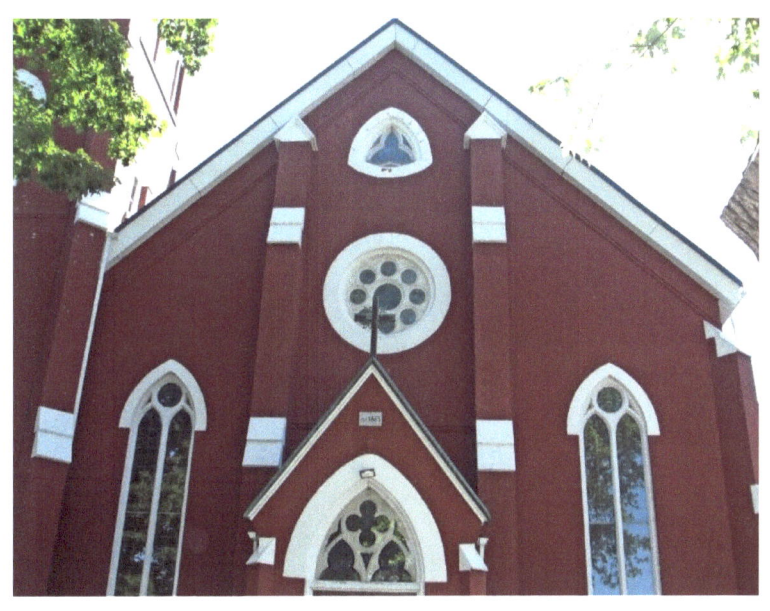

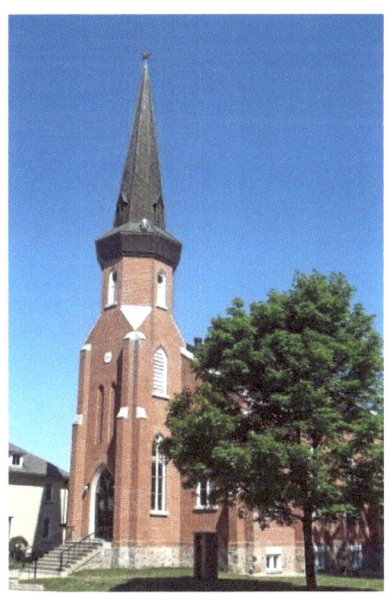

175 Queen Street East - Mount Forest United Church – 1873

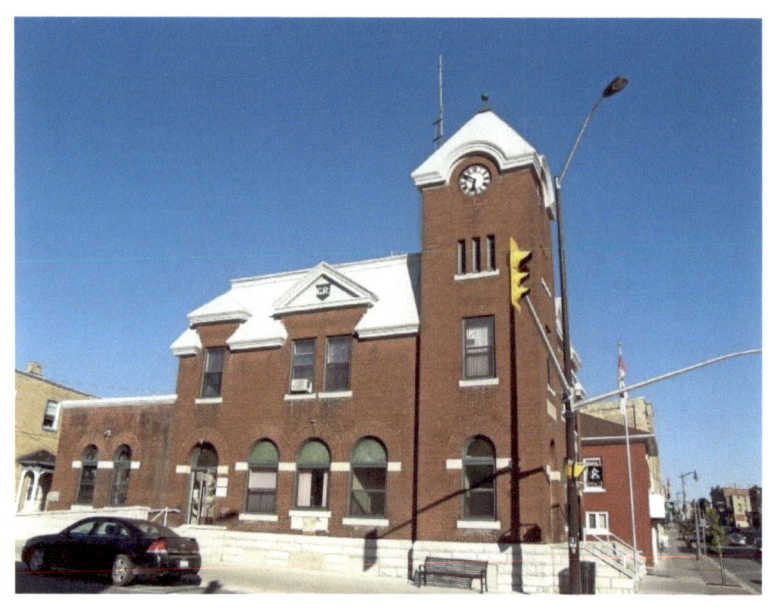

170 Wellington Street West - Mount Forest Post Office built in 1912. The timepiece for the clock tower was made in Birmingham, England.

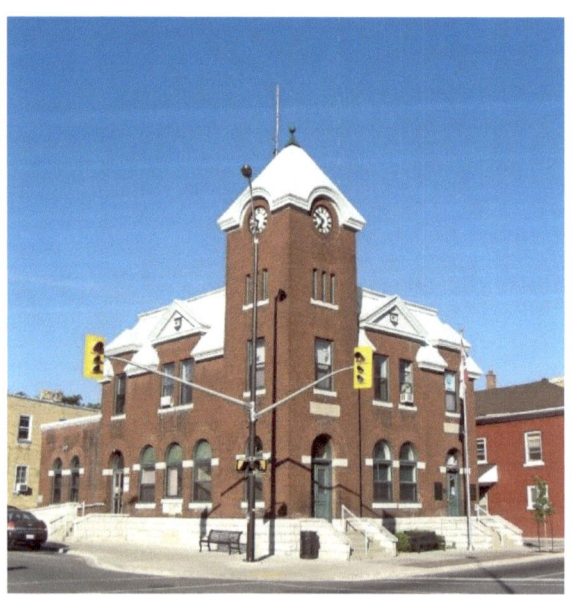

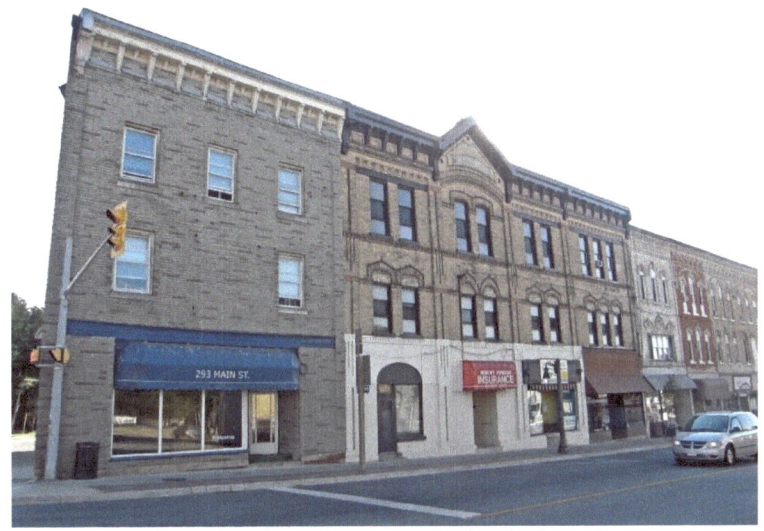

Cornice brackets, corbelled dentils

Downtown

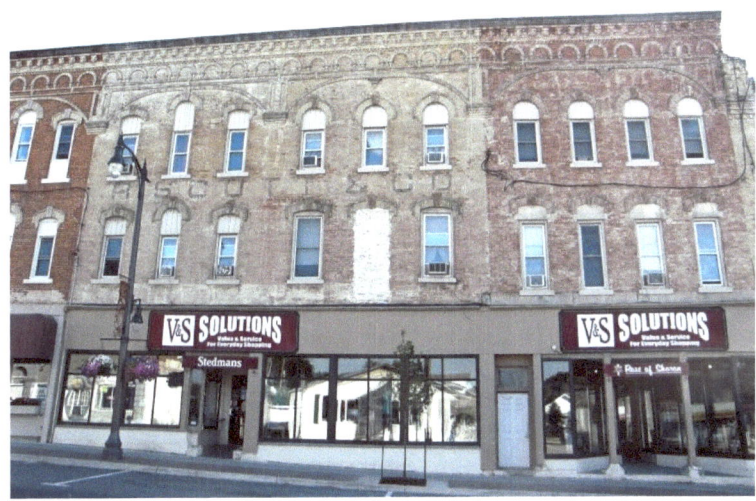

Corbelled dentils, decorative brickwork - Ascot & Company

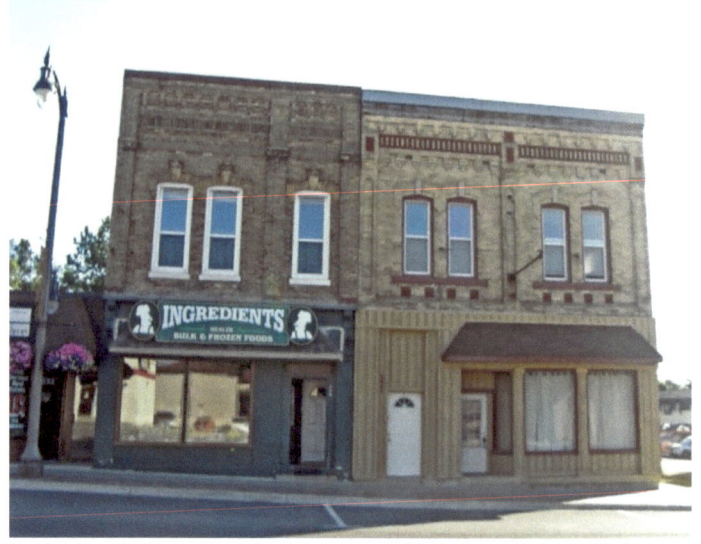

Corbelled dentils, decorative dichromatic brickwork

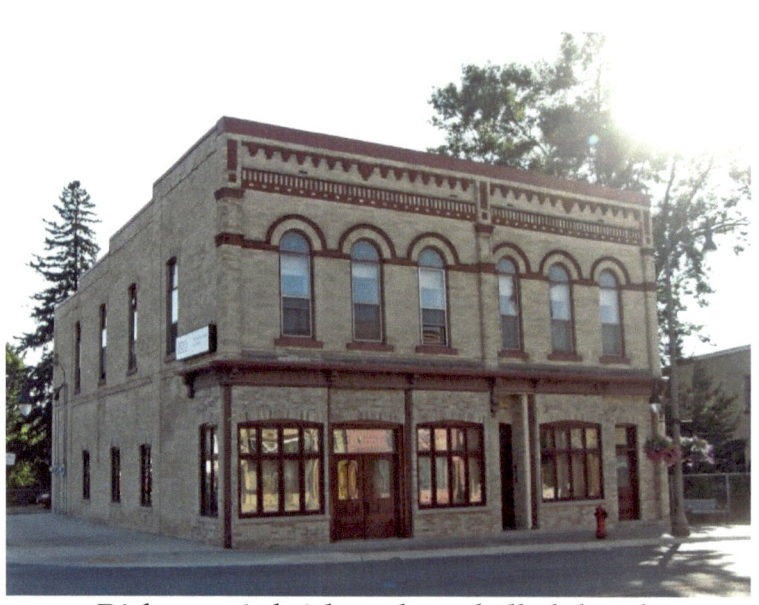

Dichromatic brickwork, corbelled dentils

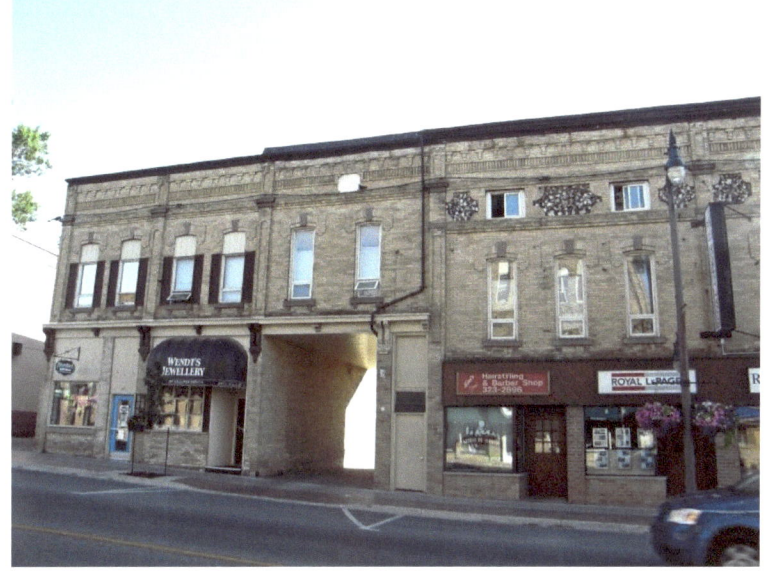

Dickson Block - 1887

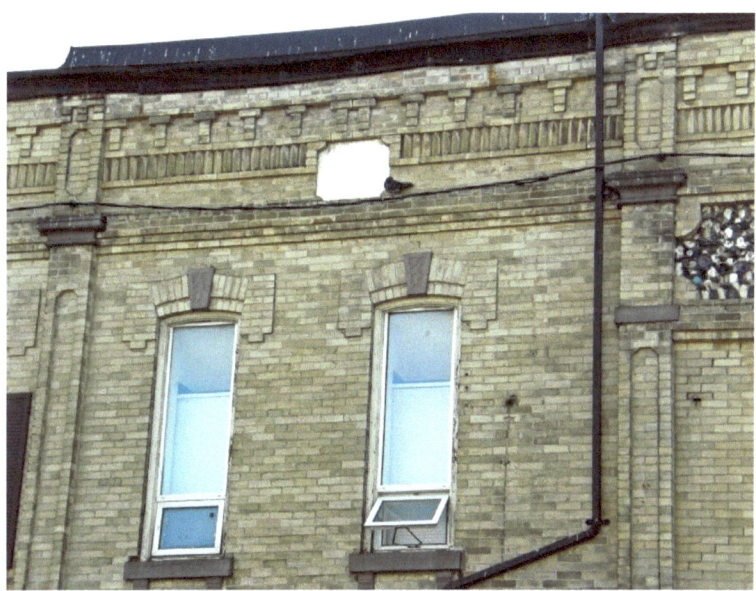

Corbelled dentils, keystones

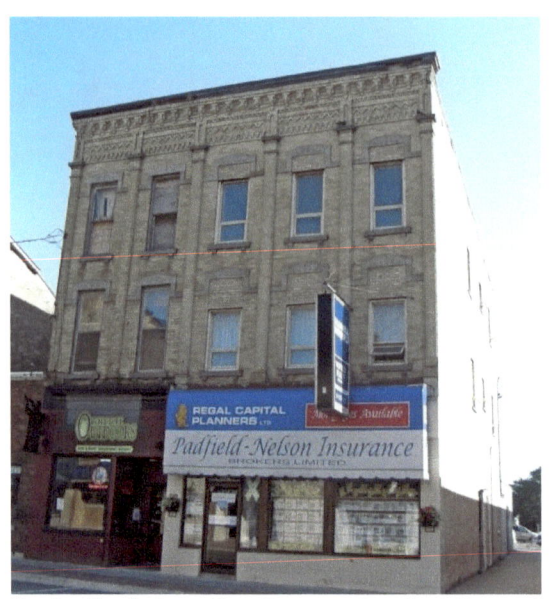

Corbelled dentils, decorative brickwork

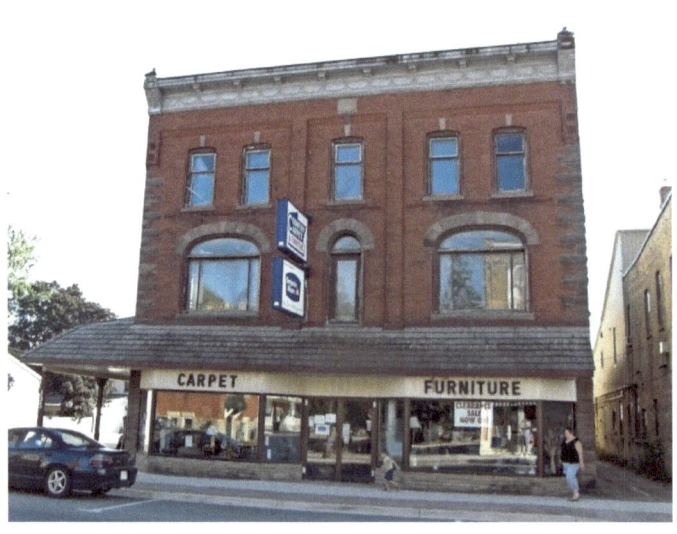

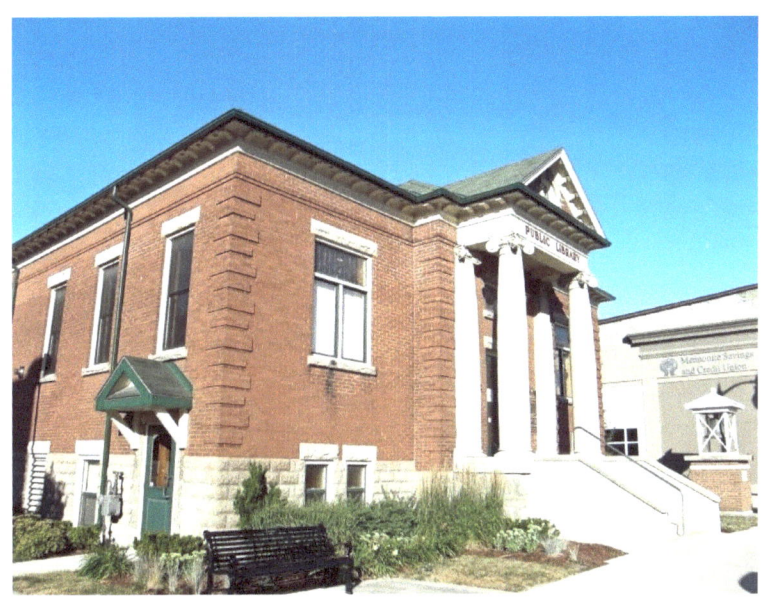

118 Main Street North - Public Library opened in 1913
Beaux Arts style

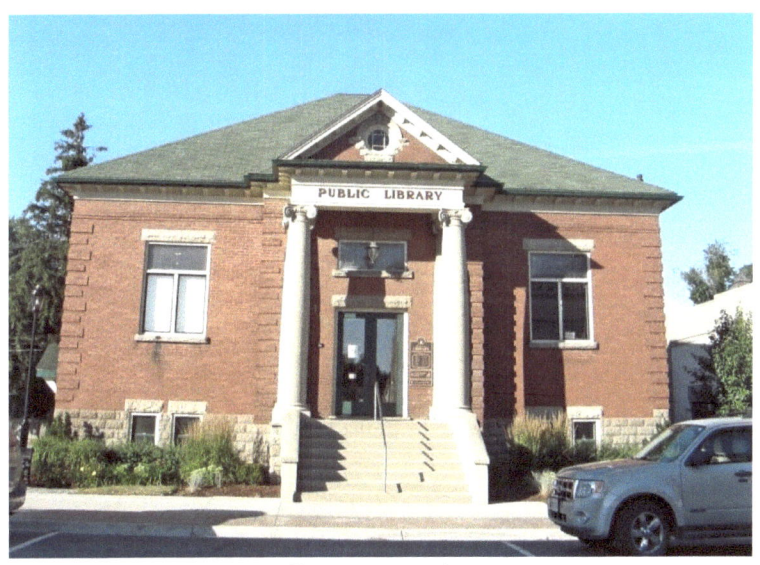

Corner quoins

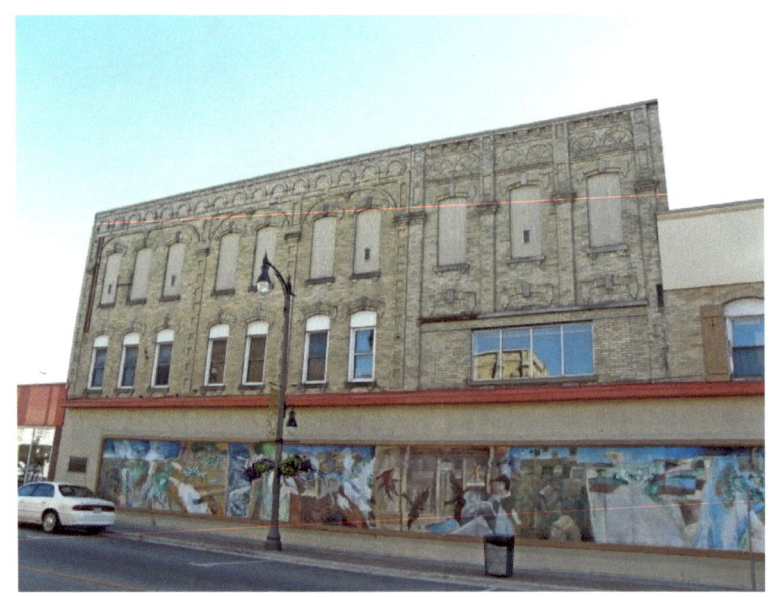

Corbelled dentils, decorative brickwork, window voussoirs with keystones, pilasters, mural on ground level

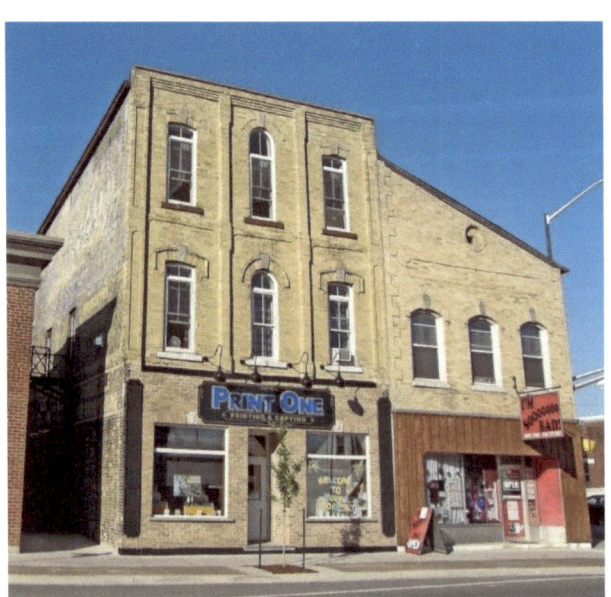

Pilasters, keystones, quoining

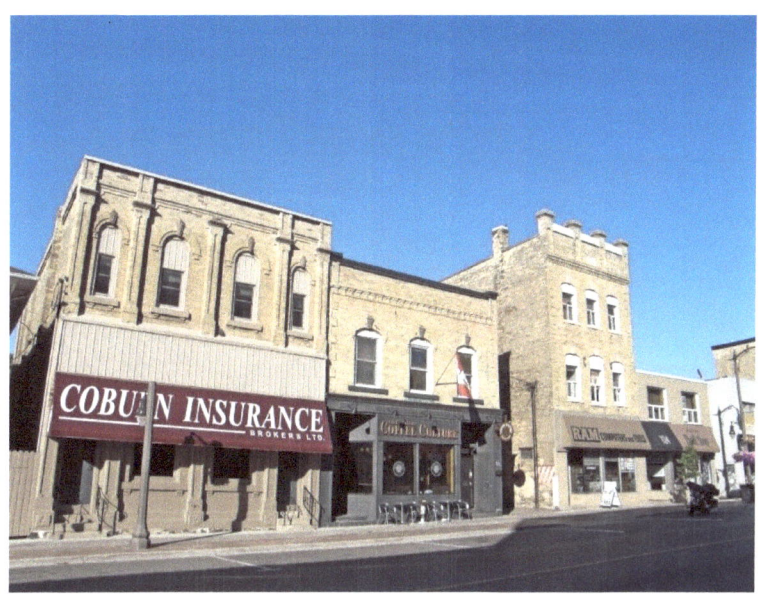

Pilasters, keystones, quoins, dentil moulding,

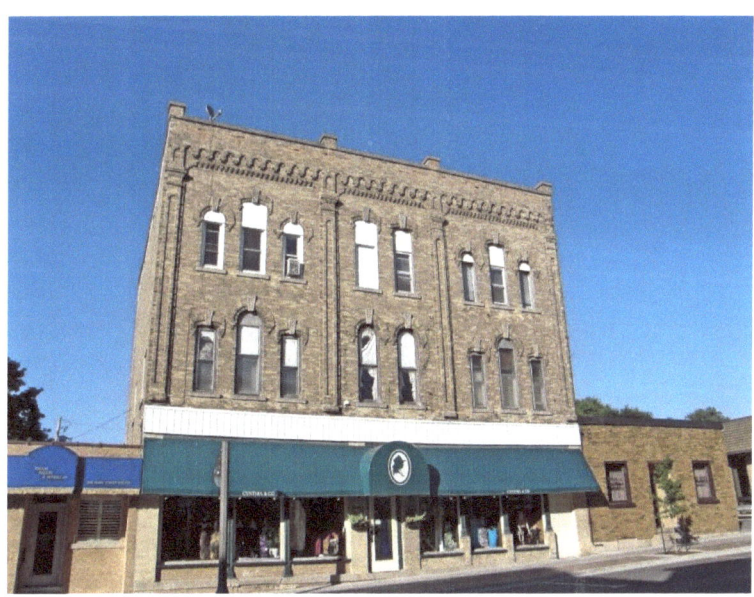

Corbelled dentils, arched voussoirs and keystones, pilasters

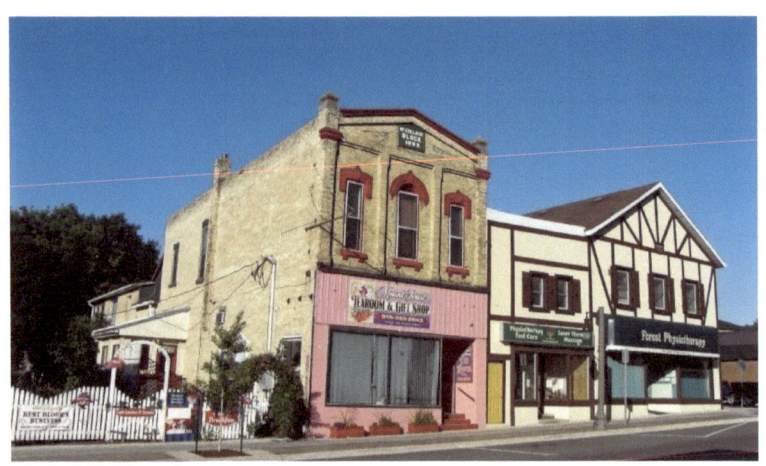

McCulloch Block – 1888 - pilasters

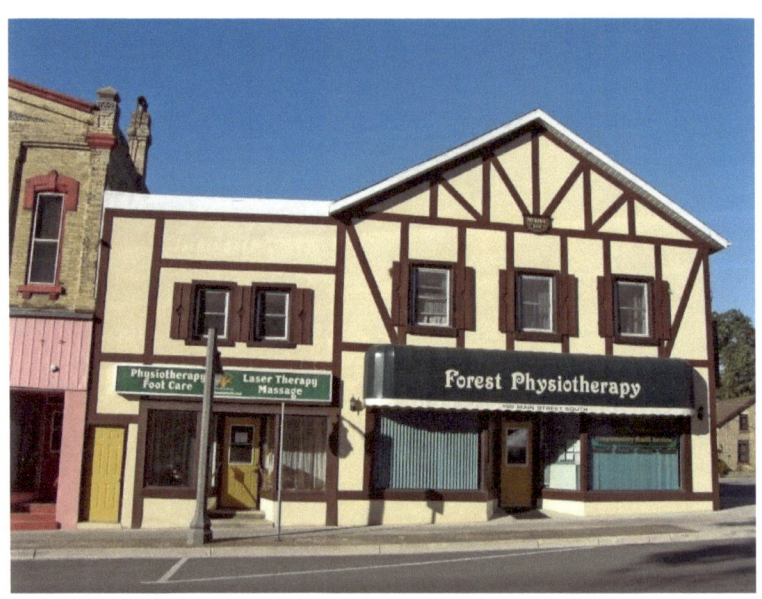

Tudor accents

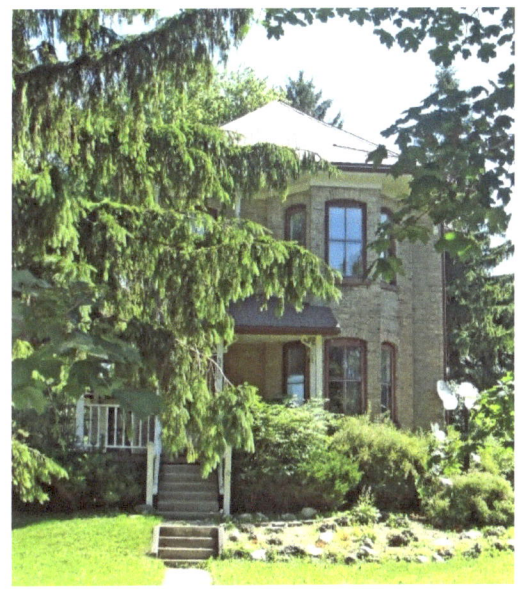

Yellow brick, two-storey bay window

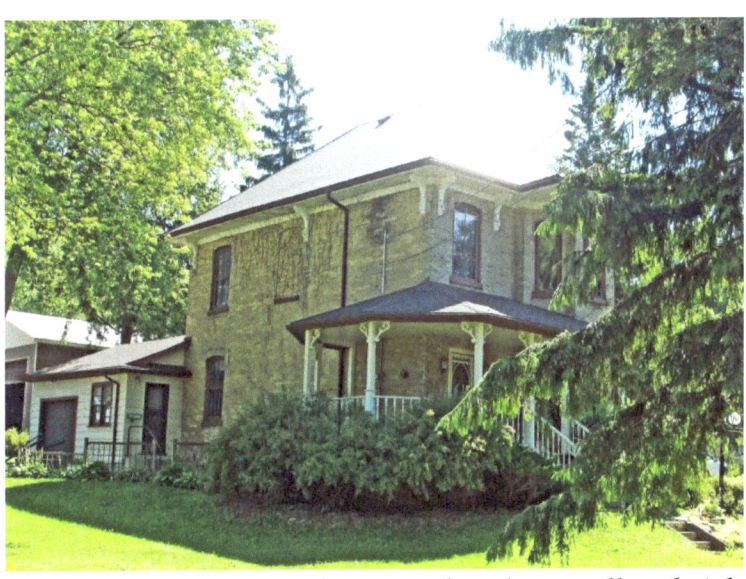

Italianate – hipped roof, cornice brackets, yellow brick

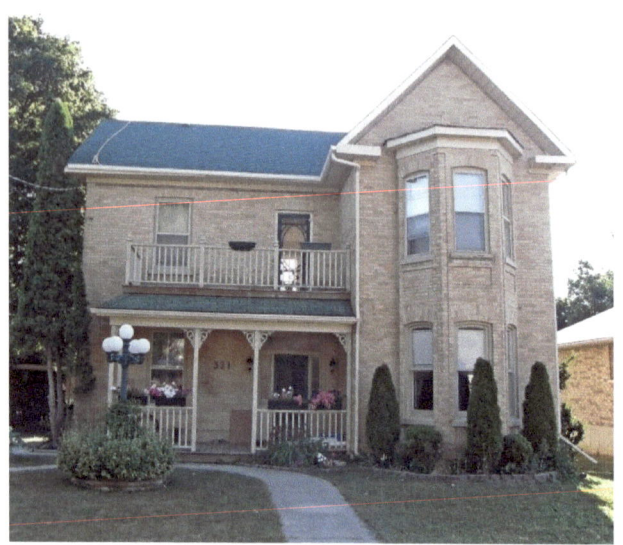

#321 – Gothic Revival, cornice return on gable,
second floor balcony

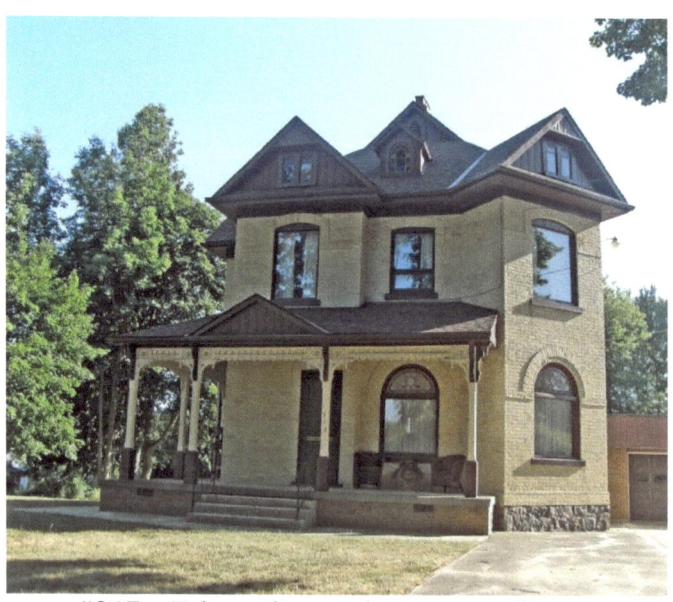

#315 – Edwardian – dormer, pediment

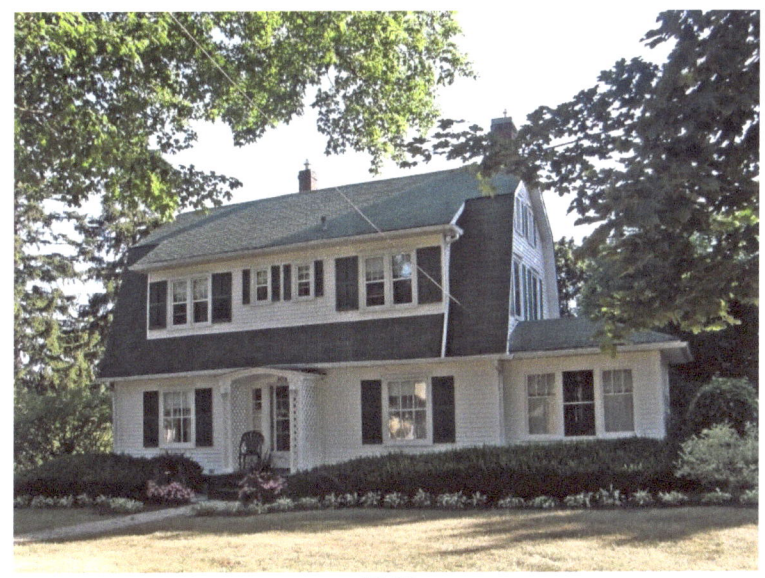

#305

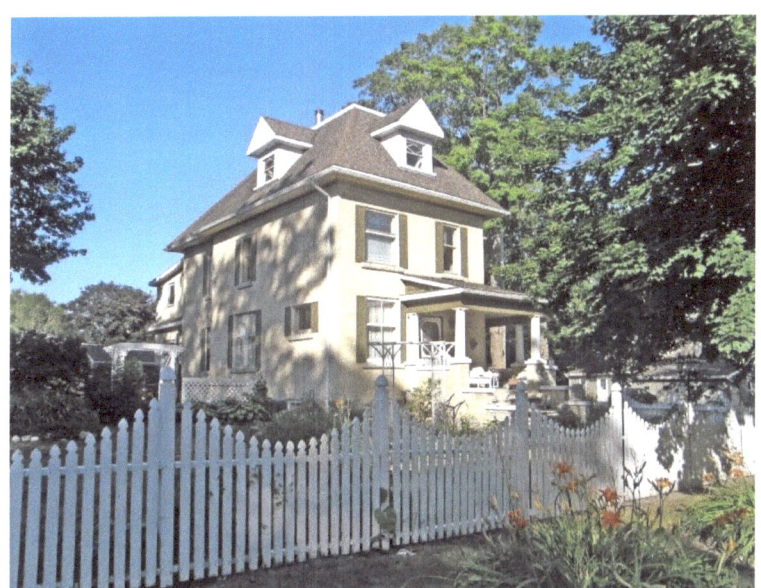

#308 – Italianate, dormers in attic, steeply pitched hip roof

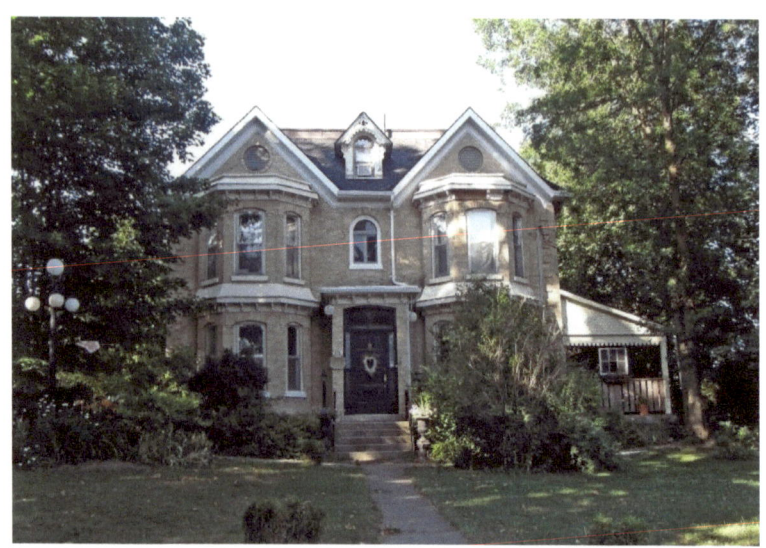

#270 – Gothic Revival, 2-storey bay windows,
dormer between gables

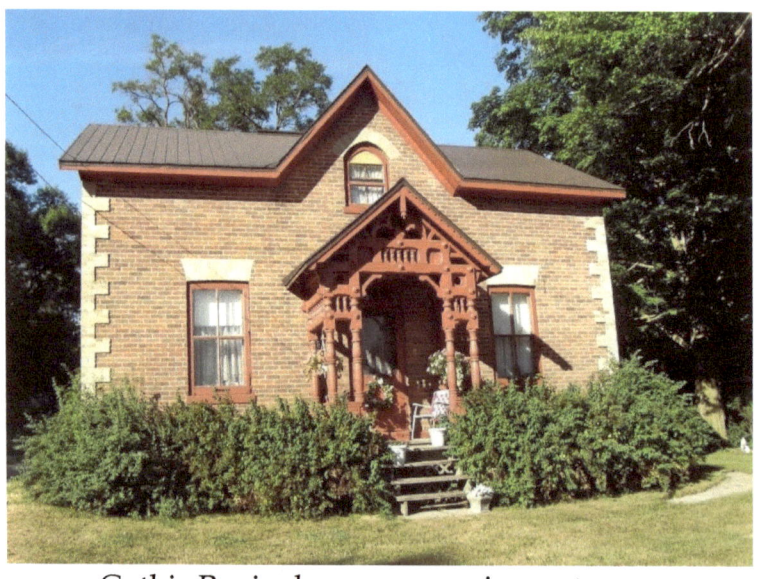

Gothic Revival – corner quoins, entrance

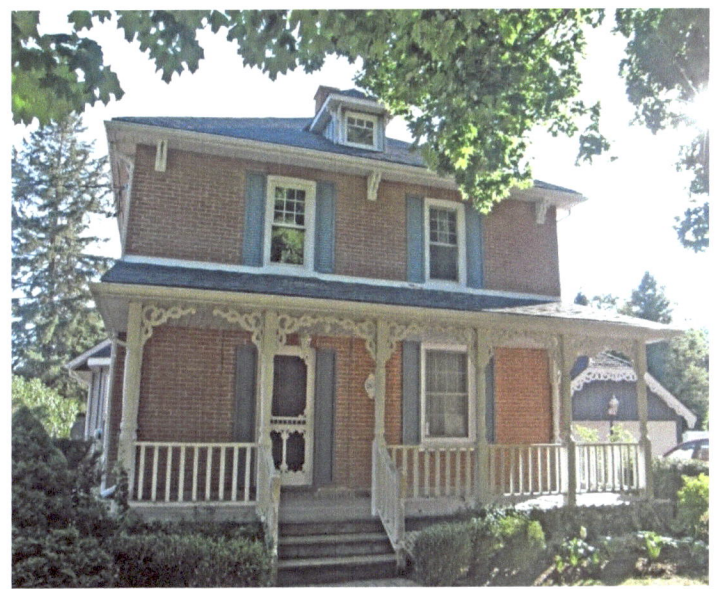

#267 – Italianate, dormer in attic

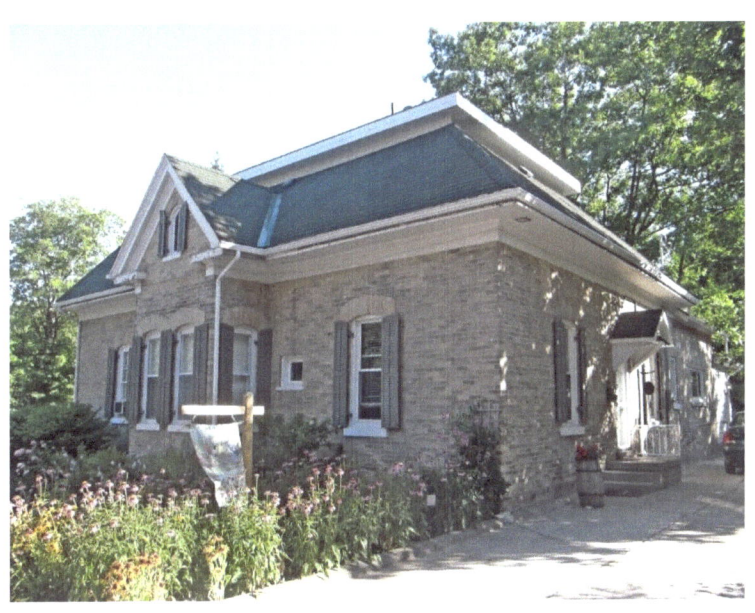

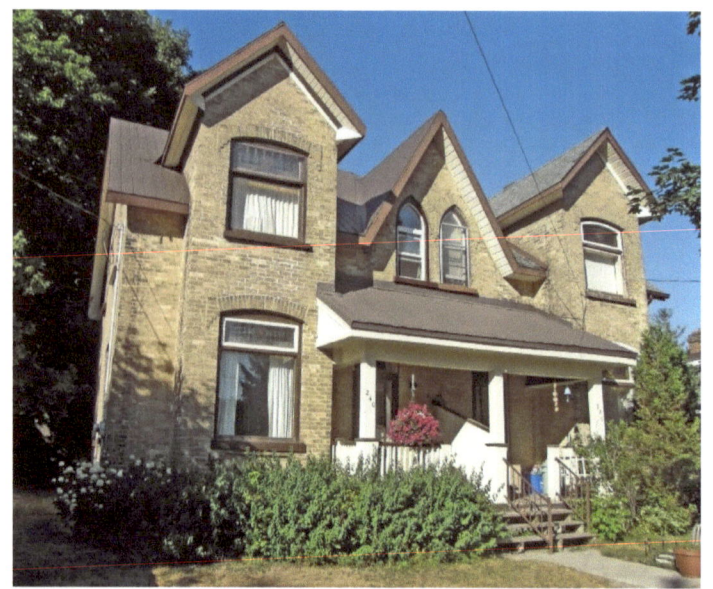

#240 – triple-gable Gothic Revival – local yellow brick

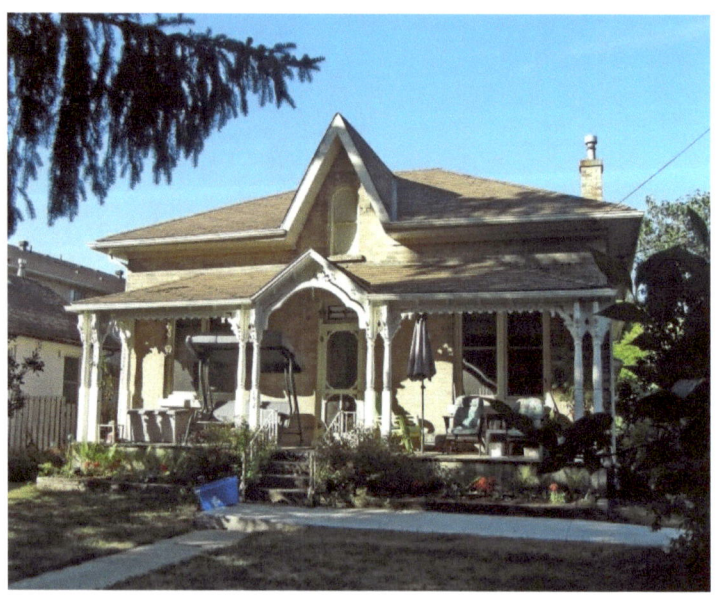

#152 – Gothic Revival

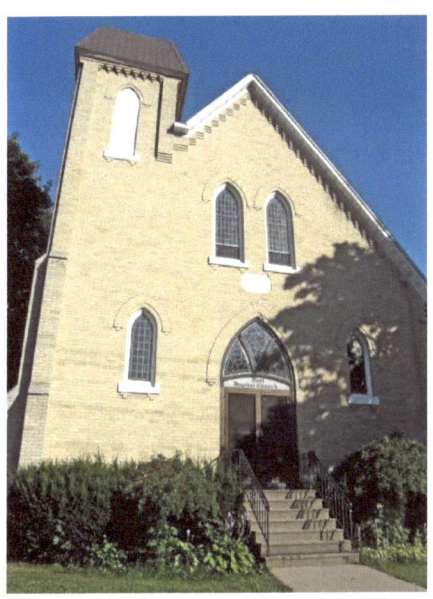

116 Fergus Street North - First Baptist Church A.D. 1884
Corbelled dentils, lancet windows, arched voussoirs

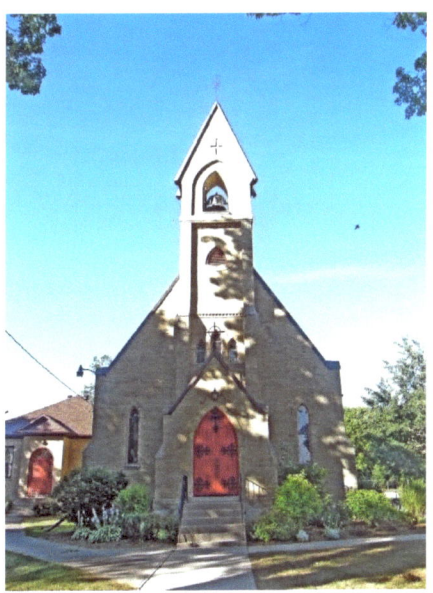

114 Fergus Street South - St. Paul's Anglican Church
Dentil moulding, lancet windows, buttresses

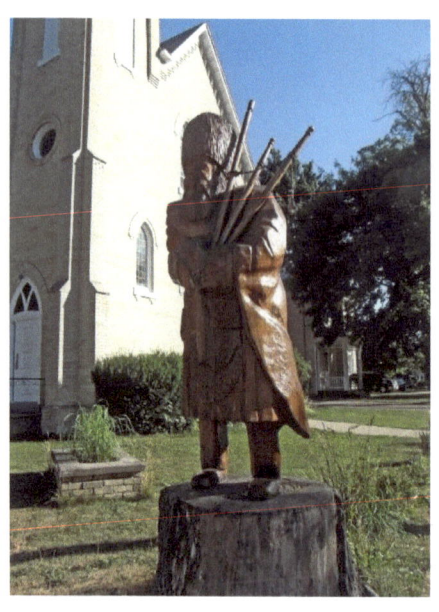

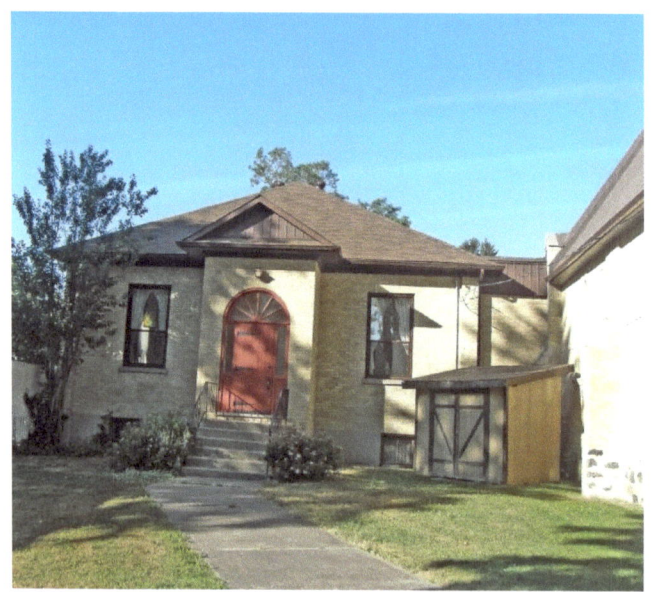

Manse beside St. Paul's Anglican Church

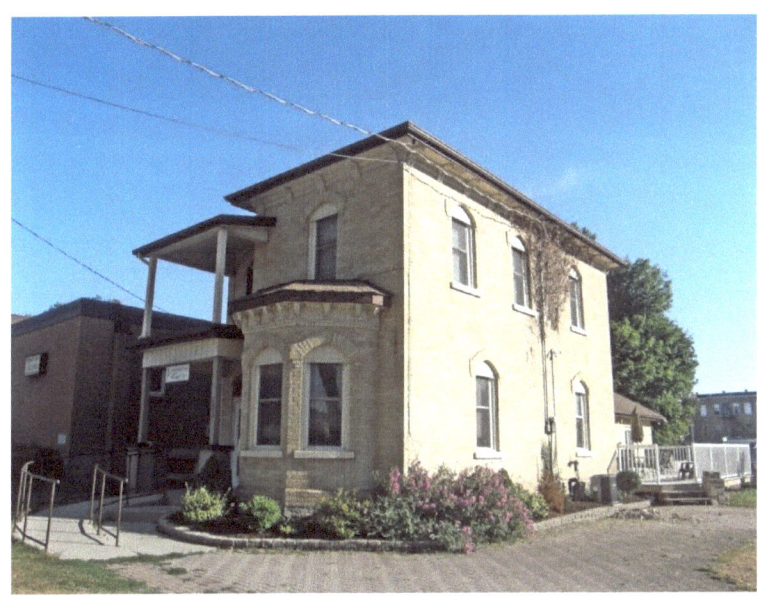

135 Wellington North - Community Living Centre
Italianate, hipped roof, bay window

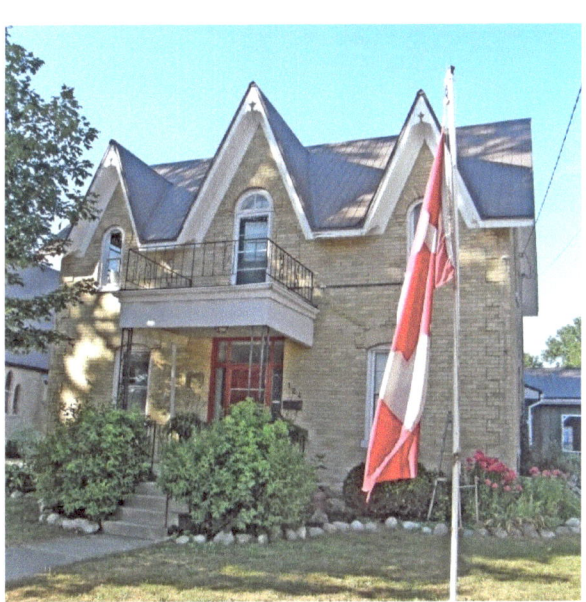

Mount Forest Centennial Home – 1879-1979
#124 – triple-gable Gothic Revival, second floor balcony

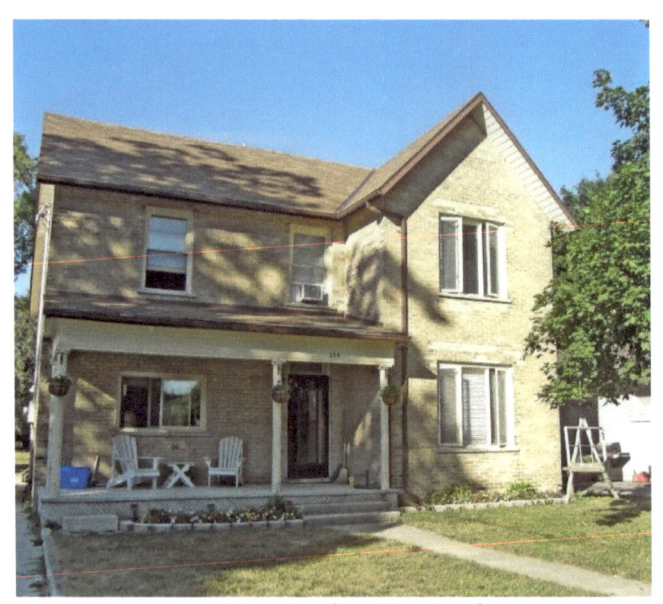

#154 – Gothic Revival
Mount Forest Centennial Home – 1879-1979

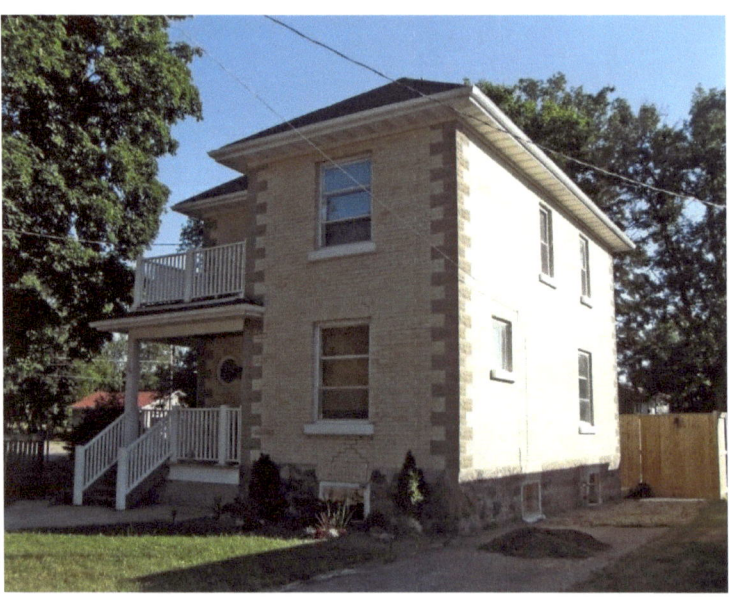

Made from local yellow brick with darker brick accents on the corner quoins

Gobles

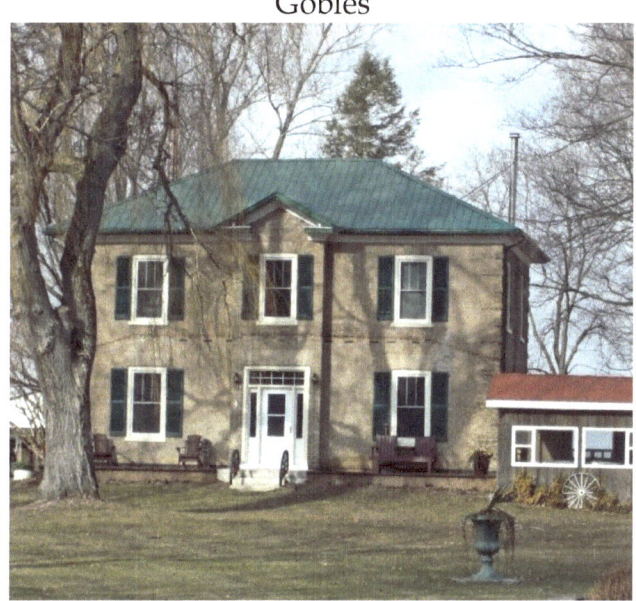

Italianate – hipped roof with two storey frontispiece

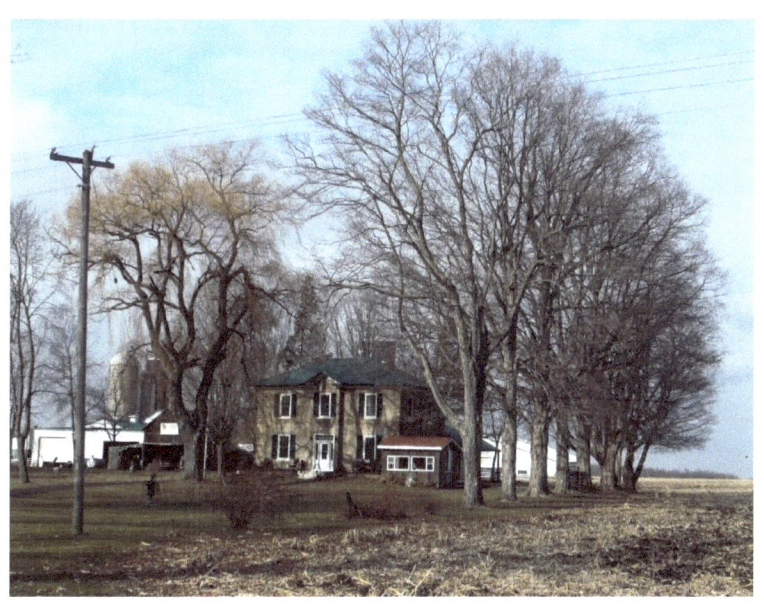

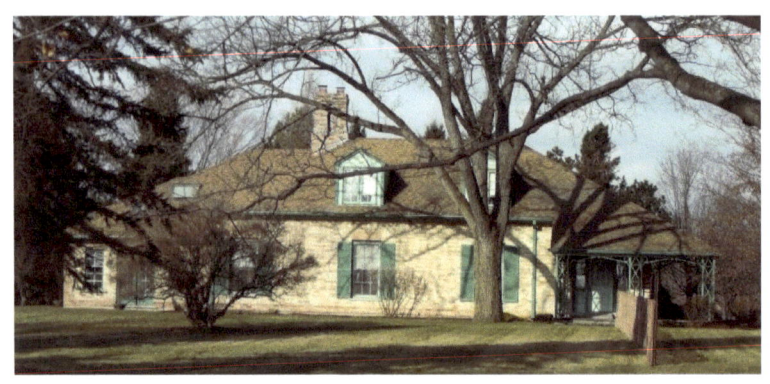

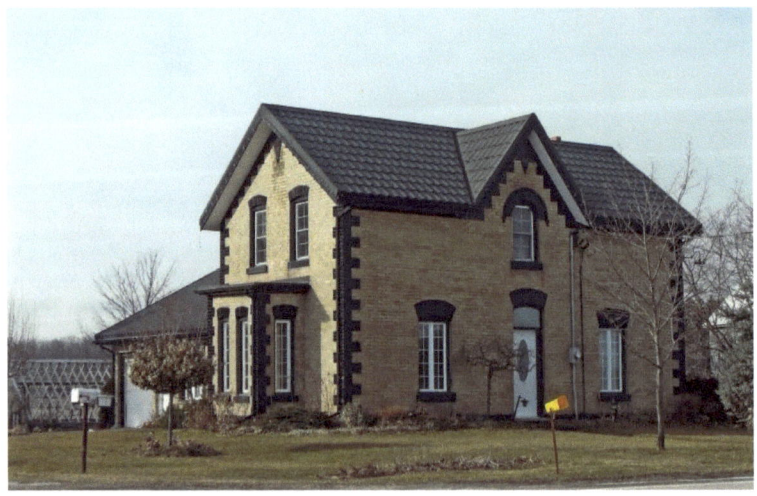

Gothic Revival, corner quoins, rectangular bay window

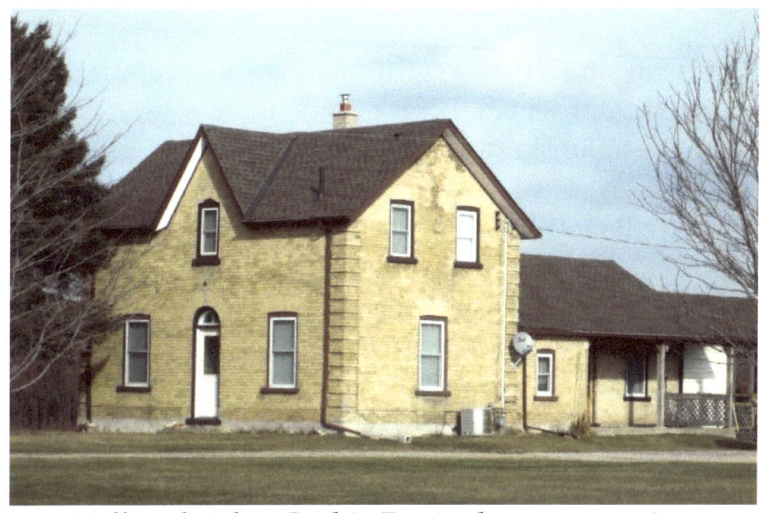

Yellow brick – Gothic Revival, corner quoins

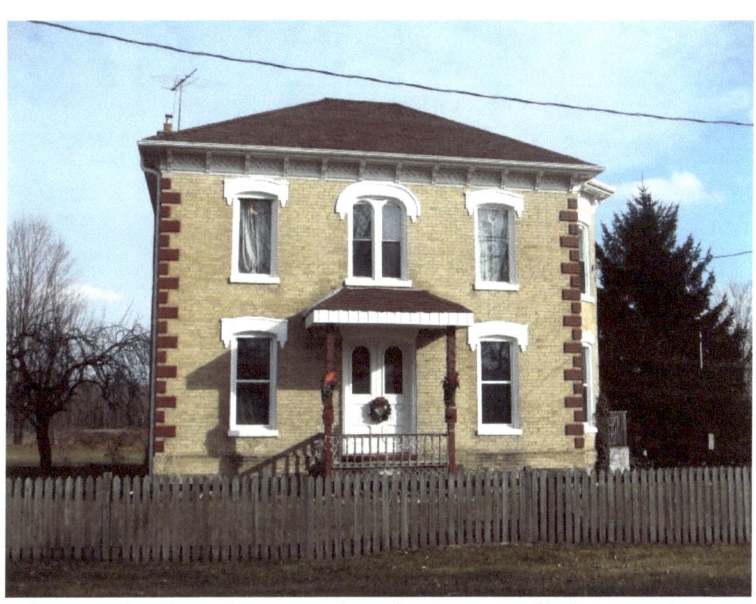

Single cornice brackets under the eaves, dichromatic toning on the corner quoins, arched window voussoirs

Brackets: a decorative or weight-bearing structural element which forms a right angle with one side against a wall and the other under a projecting surface such as an eave or roof. Example: see Page 19	
Buttress: a masonry structure built against or projecting from a wall which serves to support or reinforce the wall. In Canadian architecture, they are sometimes used for decoration. Example: see Page 8	
Capital: The uppermost finish or decoration on a column. An Ionic column has a small base, a thin elegant shaft, and a capital composed of volutes which are carved whirls or twists that take the form of a scroll. Example: Library – see Page 15	
Cornice: originally the wooden overhang of the roof. With the use of stone, brick, iron and steel, the cornice is any projecting shelf at the top of a ceiling or roof. They can be very decorative. Example: see Page 14	
Cornice Return: decorative element on the end of a gable. Example: see Page 20	
Dentil Moulding: an even series of rectangles used as ornamental decoration in cornices. Example: see Page 17	
Dichromatic brickwork: the use of two colours of brick, tile or slate to decorate a façade. Example: see Page 12	

Dormer: (French for "sleep") a gable end window that pierces through the plane of a sloping roof surface to create usable space in the top floor or attic of a building by adding headroom. Example: see Page 21	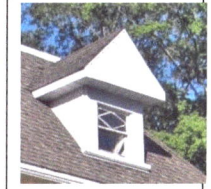
Entrance: The entrance encompasses the doorway and the inner vestibule or, in residential architecture, the covered porch. Example: see Page 22	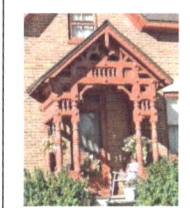
Gable: the triangular portion of a wall between the edges of a sloping roof. Example: Gobles, see Page 30	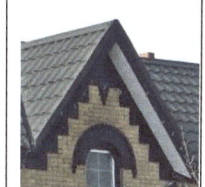
Hipped Roof: a roof where all sides slope downwards to the walls with no gables. Example: Gobles, see Page 29	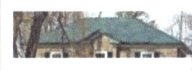
Keystones and Voussoirs: a voussoir is a wedge-shaped element used in building an arch. A keystone is the central stone that locks all the stones into position, allowing the arch to bear weight. A keystone is often enlarged and embellished. Example: see Page 17	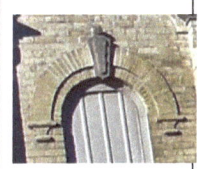
Lancet Window: a tall, narrow window with a pointed arch at its top. Example: First Baptist Church, see Page 25	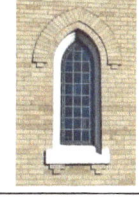

Pediment: a triangular section above the horizontal structure (entablature), typically supported by columns. The inside of the triangle is called the tympanum. Example: Library – see Page 15	
Pilaster: a slightly projecting column built into or applied to the face of a wall for additional structural support. Example: see Pages 11-14, 15-18 – downtown buildings	
Quoin: masonry blocks at the corner of a wall, often a decorative feature, usually larger or of a different colour than the rest of the wall. Example: see Page 28	
Rose Window: a circular window with ornamental tracery radiating from the centre. Example: see Page 8-9	

Building Styles

Beaux Arts: Promoters of this style sought to express the classical principles on a grand and imposing scale. Many of the Beaux Arts buildings were banks, post offices, and railway stations. The Ontario Beaux Arts style is eclectic mixing elements of Classical, Renaissance and Baroque. Often the designs have a temple-like façade, pedimented porticos, balustrades, capitals in many styles. Example: Library – see Page 15	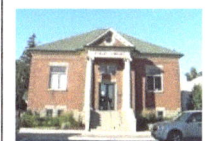
Edwardian, 1900-1930 – This style bridges the ornate and elaborate styles of the Victorian era and the simplified styles of the 20th century. Balanced facades, simple roof lines, dormer windows, large front porches, and smooth brick surfaces are its characteristics. Example: see Page 20	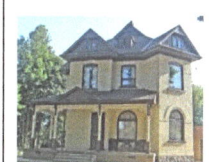
Gothic Revival, 1830-1890 – These decorative buildings have sharply-pitched gables with highly detailed verge boards, pointed-arch window openings, and dichromatic brickwork. It is a common style in Ontario. Example: see Page 24	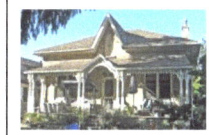
Italianate, 1850-1900 – It has wide-bracketed eaves, belvederes, wrap-around verandahs. Example: see Page 21	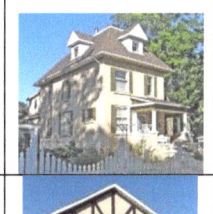
Tudor Revival – exposed timbers with stucco infill, multi-paned windows. Example: see Page 18	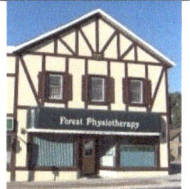